A World of Field Trips

Going to a Stadium

Rebecca Rissman

Heinemann Library
Chicago, Illinois

Edited by Rebecca Rissman, Dan Nunn, and Catherine Veitch
Designed by Richard Parker
Picture research by Tracy Cummins
Originated by Capstone Global Library Ltd
Printed and bound in China by Leo Paper Products Ltd

15 14 13 12 11
10 9 8 7 6 5 4 3 2 1

Library of Congress Cataloging-in-Publication Data
Rissman, Rebecca.
  Going to a stadium / Rebecca Rissman.
    p. cm.—(A world of field trips)
  Includes bibliographical references and index.
  ISBN 978-1-4329-6069-8 (hb)—ISBN 978-1-4329-6078-0 (pb)
1. School field trips—Juvenile literature. 2. Stadiums—Juvenile
literature. I. Title.
  LB1047.R578 2012
  371.3'8—dc22   2011015153

Acknowledgments
We would like to thank the following for permission to reproduce
photographs: Corbis pp. 6 (© Redlink), 13 (© Rolf Vennenbernd/
epa), 16 (© Kelly-Mooney Photography); Getty Images pp. 5
(Gage), 12 (Hisham Ibrahim), 15 (GOH CHAI HIN/AFP),
17 (Stephen Green/MLB Photos), 18 (Chris Graythen), 21,
23a (Kevork Djansezian), 23b (Stephen Green/MLB Photos);
Shutterstock pp. 4 (© Marek Pawluczuk), 7 (© fstockfoto), 8
© Neale Cousland), 9 (© Matt Trommer), 10 (© J. Henning
Buchholz), 11 (© Eric Broder Van Dyke), 14 (© sunxuejun), 19
(© Christopher Halloran), 20 (© L. Kragt Bakker), 22 (© Ffooter),
23c (© fstockfoto).

Front cover photograph of fans cheering the South African
National Soccer Team at the Atteridgeville stadium in Pretoria,
South Africa reproduced with permission of Getty Images (Per-
Anders Pettersson). Back cover photograph of a tennis stadium
reproduced with permission of Shutterstock (© Neale Cousland).

Every effort has been made to contact copyright holders of any
material reproduced in this book. Any omissions will be rectified
in subsequent printings if notice is given to the publisher.

Contents

Field Trips

People take field trips to see
new places.

People take field trips to learn
new things.

Field Trip to a Stadium

Some people take field trips
to stadiums.

A stadium is a place where people
go to watch sports.

Stadiums have seats for people to watch sports.

Stadiums have fields for players to play on.

Different Stadiums

Some stadiums are indoors.

The players stay dry in bad weather!

Some stadiums are outdoors.

The players feel the wind
and the Sun.

metal

Some stadiums are made of metal.

This stadium has a metal top.

wood

Some stadiums are made of wood.

This stadium has a wooden scoreboard.

Some stadiums are very big.

This big stadium has a race track.

How Should You Act at a Stadium?

Always stay with an adult at a stadium.

You can cheer loudly for your team!

What Do You Think?

What kind of stadium is this?

Look on page 24 for the answer.

Picture Glossary

cheer shout for a person or a team to succeed

scoreboard part of a stadium that shows how many points each person or team has earned

stadium place where people gather to watch sporting events

Index

Notes to Parents and Teachers

Before reading
Explain to children that a field trip is a short visit to a new place, and that it often takes place during a school day. Ask children if they have ever taken a field trip. Tell children that stadiums are where sporting events are held. Ask if any children play sports. Make a list of the sports they play on the board, and then guide children in a discussion about the different types of stadiums they may play in.

After reading
- Ask each child to draw a picture of a stadium, and then show it to the classroom. Ask the children to tell the class about their stadium, what types of sports could be played there, and if it has any special features.

Answer to page 22
It is a stadium where tennis is played.